HOW TO BE
A SUCCESSFUL
DOG

MAD®

HOW TO BE
A SUCCESSFUL
DOG

by Spot

as told to
Larry Siegel

Illustrated by
John Caldwell

Rutledge Hill Press®
Nashville, Tennessee

This book is a revised edition of *MAD's How to Be a Successful Dog,* originally published by Warner Books in 1984.

Published by Rutledge Hill Press®, Inc., 211 Seventh Avenue North, Nashville, Tennessee 37219-1823.

Distributed in Canada by H. B. Fenn & Company, Ltd., 34 Nixon Road, Bolton, Ontario L7E 1W2.

Distributed in the United Kingdom by Verulam Publishing, Ltd., 152a Park Street Lane, Park Street, St. Albans, Hertfordshire AL2 2AU.

Cover design by Sam Viviano/*MAD* Magazine
Back cover design by Consultx
Text design by Harriette Bateman
Typography by Roger A. DeLiso, Rutledge Hill Press®

Library of Congress Cataloging-in-Publication Data
Siegel, Larry, 1925–
 Mad : how to be a successful dog / by Spot, as told to Larry Siegel : illustrated by John Caldwell.
  p.   cm.
 Rev. ed. of : Mad's how to be a successful dog. 1984.
 ISBN 1-55853-784-8 (pbk.)
 1. Dogs Humor.   I. Siegel, Larry, 1925– Mad's how to be a successful dog.
II. Mad (New York, N.Y. : 1958)   III. Title.   IV. title: How to be a successful dog.
PN6231. D68S54   1999
818'.5407—dc21   99–3143
                                                             CIP

Printed in the United States of America
2 3 4 5 6 7 8 9—04 03 02 01 00 99

Contents

Introduction

So you're a young dog eager to make it in life, and you think the world out there is nothing but old slippers and Kibbles 'N Bits. You think that in order to succeed in your field all you have to do is drift along with the tide, and you're going to land in Paradise Cove. Well, you're in for a shock, kiddo, because you can do the dog paddle and still drown. That's right, a dog's life is not that simple, and you've got a lot of work cut out for you.

Let me begin by destroying a common myth: to wit, a dog functions purely by instinct. In truth just about everything you

do and will do in life (and that includes even the most mundane things such as barking, panting, and scratching your belly nine hours a day) is picked up through various learning processes. Therefore your job is to learn and mine is to teach you everything I know.

And so this book is written by a veteran dog specifically for all young dogs like yourself who are just getting started in life and eager to make a go of it. It will educate, edify, and enlighten you in all of the fine points of dogdom, and will demonstrate that the difference between being a dog and being a *successful* dog is like the difference between being Miss Fetzler, a third-grade math teacher, and being Albert Einstein (and since many dogs *look* like Einstein, that should be incentive enough).

MAD®

HOW TO BE
A SUCCESSFUL
DOG

Knowing Who You Are

As a fledgling dog growing up in the highly unpredictable new millennium, it is very easy to develop an immediate and deadly inferiority complex. Just hop over to any bookstore, or let your paws do the walking through the best-seller pages. In fact I've just pawed through them.

You know what you'll find among the top three favorite book subjects of our time? Cats! That's right. Cats, cats, and more cats.

Cat books sell in the millions. For some reason the public just can't get enough of Garfield, the musical play *Cats*, and the rest of those feline freaks. As for dog books . . . Well, I figure this one will sell about nine copies (unless the publisher happens to send a free one to my master, in which case—make it eight).

That's pretty heavy stuff to swallow, particularly when you're just getting started in a dog's world. So what are you going to do about it? Whimper and throw yourself in front

of a runaway pit bull? Don't be ridiculous! Suicide solves nothing for a young dog, and you've got too much living ahead of you.

But first things first. To be a successful dog (and believe me, you can do it despite the best-seller lists), you must establish your identity in your own mind and never let it go. If you know who you are at all times and don't try to be anything else, the rest is relatively easy. Don't forget: You're man's best friend, not a *man*. And certainly not a cat.

To begin with, if dogs and cats were cities, we would be New York and they would be Los Angeles. Let me explain that concept to you.

Just like the Big Apple, we dogs are excitable, vitriolic entities. We're emotional, visceral, and like the traffic at Columbus Circle, we always seem to be dashing around in ten different directions.

Watch one of your older brothers some time as he greets his master by rolling over, wagging his tail like a runaway pendulum, and panting so hard you think his heart is going to explode. He seems to be saying, "Oh, boy, am I glad to see *you* again! I thought you'd never come back [*pant pant*]!

Wow, you haven't changed a bit [*wag wag*]! You're still my beloved master, and I'll always love you and be loyal to you until the day I die [*roll roll*]! Only, please, for the love of God, don't ever leave me like that again [*wag wag . . . pant pant*]! *Ever . . . ever . . . !* You promise???" (And that's when his master has just come back from the bathroom.)

As for cats, well, as I said, now you're dealing with Los Angeles. The key expression here is "mellow and laid-back." Nothing ever excites or fazes cats. They're as boring and changeless as a sunny, smoggy, 85 degree day on Wilshire Boulevard.

All cats do is sidle and slink. They're so indifferent and nonchalant they can make you sick. Watch a cat greet his owner some time. You can almost hear him saying, "Hey, dude, what's happening [*sidle sidle*]? You're lookin' good, baby [*slink slink*]. I'm cool, you know what I mean [*sidle sidle*]? Anyway, have a nice day, ya hear [*slink slink*]?" (And that's during an earthquake!)

Okay, now I'm going to tell you something that should make your day, if not your whole life. In essence, we dogs are true pets—cats are impostors. That's right, you heard me. Etch that on your brain with an electric pencil. Cats are impostors!

What is a cat doing while we're loyally earning our keep by never being more than eleven inches from our master's side? He's out in a back alley somewhere doing God-knows-what with God-knows-who!

Oh, sure, lots of people say they have cats, but nobody really *owns* one. How can you own something that spends 95 percent of his time in the street—and the infinitesimal

time he spends *in* the house, he's as warm and affectionate as a trash compactor?

So remember at all times that you're a dog, and be proud of it. Also remember that I'm writing this book because I love my fellow dogs: I don't believe we get a fair shake in life, and I hope to elevate newcomers like you once and for all to the exalted position we so eminently deserve. (Of course, the mere fact that this chapter just gave me an idea for writing a sensational new cat book shouldn't concern you in the least. What's wrong with making a small fortune on the side while you're engaged in a labor of love?)

The Importance of Cute

A wise biped once said that for anyone to be successful in this world he (or she) must learn to do two basic, interrelated things:

1. Come up with a commodity.
2. Learn how to sell it.

Whether it's a short route to the Indies, a whole life insurance policy, a pair of terrific legs, or an automatic flush toilet, the principle is the same: Get it out there, sell it, and you've got it made.

As dogs we've got only *one* thing to sell: "cute." And don't you ever forget it. Sure, we've all heard of those cliché qualities that supposedly endear a dog to his master, like being man's best friend, having undying loyalty, and so on. But the fact remains that 99 percent of the time all they really want from us is what they want from a six-month-old infant: pure, unadulterated *cute*! And if in time we happen to move up to "adorable," that's just more icing on the cake.

But before you get too smug about it, remember this: They're stuck with the kid no matter what kind of clod he may grow up to be.

As for dogs, let up on your cuteness just once, and

either you'll find a For Sale sign around your neck or, in more extreme cases (depending on your age), they may resort to that dreaded practice known euphemistically as "putting you to sleep."

In case you're unfamiliar with the term, let me see if I can explain it as gently as possible: you know how we dogs usually spend twenty hours of every day napping? Well, make that twenty-four and tack on the word "forever" after "napping."

However, cute can be a tricky word, and it's important to know exactly what is cute and what isn't. So pay careful attention to the following, keeping in mind that this is a mere handful out of the thousands of situations that will arise in your life.

What's Cute and What's Not Cute

Bringing your master his slippers in your mouth is cute.
Bringing your master some dog doo in your mouth is *not* cute.

Rolling over on your back and wagging your tail in a demonstration of total submission is cute.
Bending over to lick your private parts is *not* cute.

Burying an old bone somewhere out in the back is cute.

Burying an old bone in a hole in the living room rug (particularly when there was no hole in the rug before you started burying it) is *not* cute.

Licking your master's feet is cute.

Licking your master's socks can be cute, depending on how old they are.

Licking your master's socks while they're on his feet is

never cute, no matter how old they are (the socks *or* the feet).

Sleeping on the floor at your master's side is cute.
Sleeping in your master's bed is also cute, particularly if he can't stand his wife and you sleep between them.
Sleeping in your master's bed if he's there with his mistress is certainly not cute (which you'll find out for

yourself when he drop-kicks you across the room, out the window, and into a rhododendron plot in the garden).

Choosing the Right Master

With slavery officially dead in this country for well over a hundred years now, I realize the expression "master" is a bit demeaning to a free spirit like yourself. But a master is a fact of life, and you need one in yours. After all, you don't want to spend the rest of your days in a pet shop! You certainly don't want to wind up in a pound, and running

loose in the streets is a risky and unsatisfying business—
dining al fresco does have its charming moments, but take
it from one who knows, when you've seen one garbage can
you've seen them all.

So, a master it is, and if you're lucky enough to choose
the right one, life can be beautiful. Oh, yes, make no mistake about it, you have as much to say about picking one
as an owner does in selecting you.

As I mentioned in the previous chapter, the number
one weapon at your command is cute. So, if the person

contemplating buying you seems the least bit hesitant and—this is very important—*you're interested in the transaction*, turn the cute faucets on full blast.

An important tip: The one aspect of cute they're most interested in when purchasing a dog is—excuse the old-fashioned expression—"pep." The more movement and kinetic fury you can demonstrate, the more receptive they are. So, when they confront you, pull out all the stops. If you're familiar with the Cirque du Soleil circus troupe, give them a minor, canine "running and jumping" version of the act; also wag your tail like the blades of a helicopter, pant like a water buffalo in heat, and lick every part of them you can possibly get your tongue on. I guarantee you an immediate sale.

By the same token, if someone seems interested in you but you're less than thrilled, give them the reverse treatment. Put yourself in low gear, shlump a lot around the

floor, sigh mournfully, and look painfully sad as if you're a walking repository of *weltschmerz*. A word of warning: An excessively sad look comes very close sometimes to bordering on cute, so don't overdo it. (For example, notice George Costanza's doleful look on *Seinfeld*. He may have been partly responsible for killing his fiancée, but you must admit he was cute.)

It's also a good idea to whine and wheeze a lot. Wheezing is particularly effective, especially if you add a slight whistle to your snort. This will give the impression that you're seriously ill. And if there's one thing humans avoid like the plague in a pet, it's the plague!

It's not always easy to pick out a desirable master. You'll have to rely on that old yardstick: gut instinct. If the chemistry is right, you'll know it. But assuming your ambition is to have a ball in life while contributing only a minimum of effort, you'll have no trouble whatsoever spotting the turkeys, whom you should avoid at all cost.

Here are three choice types to keep away from:

1. The Obedience Nut

As a pet owner, this character's sole purpose in life is to transform you into a robot. For some weird reason the Obedience Nut thinks you were put on earth as a Nazi storm trooper clone. The man is obviously dangerous, and the most important word in

his vocabulary is "Heel!" (which you must admit is very close to *"Heil!"*).

He feels that if he can get you to sit nine inches from his right foot whenever he gives the command, it's a feat somewhat analogous to finding a permanent cure for sickle cell anemia. One of his more nauseating obedience techniques is the "carrot and stick" approach. In this case the carrot being a lousy dog biscuit if you obey, and the stick being a lash sharply across your flanks if you don't. As one who's eaten more than a few of my owner's jaw-shattering biscuits, I may soon be the first dog in history to have a partial dental plate in my mouth. Believe me— you're better off with the stick.

2. The Physical Culture Kook

There is alive in our land today a certain kind of maniac who not only is a body fitness slave, but (and here's where the true horror comes in) insists on including his dog in his idiotic daily regimen. So you can see him at 4:30 in the morning not only punishing his feet on the pavement in an excruciating ten-mile run, but—God help us—dragging his dog along with him at the end of a leash. You need him like triple bypass surgery.

3. The Dog Show Fetishist

This could also be a man, but it's usually a middle-aged woman. Her ambition is to make a—ugh!—show dog out of you. Which includes grooming you, washing and brushing you, and putting—yecch—rollers in your coat the way

she puts them on her head. (Do you know how painful that can be if you're a Mexican hairless? But the fetishist will do it anyway.)

The object of all this torture is to get you to prance around at a kennel club competition, win some ribbons, use you to help breed champion dogs, then watch thousands of dollars roll in. And guess who gets to keep all the money? (A hint: When was the last time you saw a Merrill Lynch stock portfolio or a municipal bond or a money market account made out to "Rover"?)

Those Vital Daily Walks

Let's assume you've chosen your master, you're safely ensconced in your new home, and you've proven yourself worthy in the important art of cute. (Note: If you happen to be a bulldog, there's no way you can ever be cute, so you'll have to prove yourself in other ways. However, if you're a Great Dane, you never have to prove *anything*.) At any rate, now that you're totally accepted by the family, and you're all warm and cozy and happy in your house, what's the first thing that should be on your mind? Exactly. Finding a way to get out. And there are—as is true in

every facet of life—correct and incorrect ways to handle this.

For instance, you can patiently wait for your three standard daily walks—the 7:00 A.M. jaunt, the noon romp, and the postprandial evening stroll. If you're willing to accept this kind of schedule as your sole means of egress, that's your privilege. But may I make a small suggestion: put this book down and go find one called *How to Be a Dog*. You're apparently not interested in becoming a *successful* one.

By the way, if you happen to live in a house with a "doggie door," which affords you free in-and-out access to

the backyard, skip this chapter, since you will obviously never go for a walk for the rest of your life. The doggie door is a convenience for lazy masters who pride themselves in having life under total control by eliminating a major responsibility—walking the dog.

Now for the proper method of negotiating an unscheduled walk. First of all, you must choose the propitious moment for both you and your master. Generally the ideal time for you is when you have insomnia—i.e., you've just gotten up after seventeen hours of sleep and for some strange reason you can't fall asleep again, and there's just nothing else to do. The best time for your owner (as far as *you're* concerned) is when he's nestled in his living room

chair, it's sudden death overtime in the Super Bowl, and there's a blinding snowstorm outside.

You are now ready for your first move. Seize your leash with your teeth, approach him, and affect two of your more minor "cute" poses: the quizzical look and the slow tail wag. His response will more than likely be: "Oh, God, I took you out an hour ago. Don't bug me."

But don't be discouraged. This is merely a preliminary gesture on your part, and you don't have to expect success with it. What you're really doing is laying the groundwork for the *coup de grâce*. And here it comes:

You slither over to the front door, drop to the floor, and then proceed to vocalize your feelings. With some loud, healthy barks, right? Wrong! You bark all day at the cable guy, the mailman, Jehovah's Witnesses, etc. Chances are your master won't even acknowledge you, or will yell something like, "Quiet, boy, or I'll belt you one!"

When I say vocalize your feelings, I'm alluding to that one canine throat emanation that cannot be ignored by *any* dog owner. The sound that turns women to quivering blobs of Jell-O and men to palsied human rubbish. I'm referring, of course, to the plaintive whimper.

A word about this because it could very well be one of the key weapons in your entire arsenal. If you learn to whimper correctly, utilizing proper tonal and pitch varia-

tions, you are guaranteed to not only get him out of his chair but move the French out of Paris.

He will now walk over to you, and here is where the battle of wits begins. A battle, which I'm delighted to tell you, you can't lose. He knows that you tended to your business an hour ago, and in his heart of hearts he may be positive that you're faking now, but on the slim chance that you're not, he's got much more at stake than you. So as far as you're concerned, all systems are go. And since he doesn't know your system, he realizes you'd *better* go.

When going for a walk (be it scheduled or nonscheduled), the first rule to remember is:

You *must* sniff *everything*.

So, as soon as your first paw makes contact with the outside air, you begin immediately by sniffing the door-mat. From there you move along sniffing the ground, then the mailbox, then on to inhaling the bricks on the side of the house. Next you sniff the mortar between the bricks, then the holes in the mortar between the bricks, then the bugs in the holes in the mortar. Then you move on to grass, rocks, sticks, mud, nails, and so on.

Quick Quiz: *How will you know when it's time to stop sniffing and move on to other activities?*

Answer: When your nose is one inch away from a fresh dog deposit, your mouth is open, your collar suddenly snaps like a hangman's noose, and you find your-self dangling from the end of your leash, three feet off the ground, gasp-ing for breath and kicking violently at the air.

Once the sniffing phase of your walk is concluded, you have your choice of many other exciting things to do: growling and barking at passing joggers is always fun; so is rolling over on the grass to dislodge fleas (statistical note: the average single grass roll will enable you to lose approximately 148 fleas . . . and pick up 212 ticks).

Here is an important piece of advice. Whatever you do outside, never—allow me to repeat—*never* engage in that

most senseless of all traditional canine activities: chasing cats. Here are three reasons why:

1. Cats are faster than we are.
2. Cats are smarter than we are.
3. Cats are agile and nimble, and they can climb to places we never even knew existed, while we—and we might as well face facts—are basically klutzes.

But aside from these reasons and five more I could mention but won't (I believe you've suffered enough), let's assume that you are destined to make the *Guinness Book of World Records* by being the first dog to actually catch a cat. Before you do go out and accomplish this small miracle, ask yourself: Once I have a cat, what am I going to do with it?

For one thing, cats are too tough to eat. For another, you certainly don't want to play with them. You two have absolutely nothing in common. Besides, cats are neatness freaks, and I guarantee you they'll drive you up the wall with such peculiarities as their meticulous ablutions and their fastidious toilet habits.

Speaking of toilet habits, you must be aware of course that as far as your owner is concerned, that is the *only* reason for *any* of your walks. So if your sole *raison d'être* as a dog is to receive asinine rewards like a pat on the head and the words "good boy" as soon as you hit the bricks, you'll dutifully spray the side of a tree and take a quick squat in the grass. And then you'll find yourself back in the house so fast, your empty head will swim. No, I expect better things from you, and I like to think that you expect better things from yourself.

In the game of "taking a walk," we always hold two key trump cards. Use both your functions wisely, spreading them out as long as possible. Remember, the catchwords are "delay, delay, delay."

Once you use Number One, hold on to Number Two for dear life. You've done it before, for hours, in the house. There's no reason that you can't do it outdoors—on *your* time.

A final word on the subject before going on to other matters. For a successful dog, attending to bodily functions is an acquired art, just like everything else. And for that reason, once you are ready to make your big move, it is imperative that you observe one paramount rule: You *must* find "the right spot."

Even the greenest, most unworldly dog knows that you don't make your deposit just anywhere. What some may want to know is, How do you find the "right spot"? My answer is simply this: How does a pachyderm find the graveyard of lost elephants? How do the swallows know how and when to return to Capistrano?

Trust me, you'll know it when you see it. True, it may take some time, and it might involve subjecting both you and your owner to a drenching downpour or other vicissitudes of nature. But God put it out there somewhere for us, and under no circumstances should we settle for a poor substitute.

Once you do find *the* spot, you must follow these important steps:

1. Approach it judiciously.
2. Circle it carefully.
3. Hover over it for at least three to five minutes (think of a jet in a holding pattern over O'Hare in Chicago).
4. Then you hit it.

Remember this (you may want to save it as your life-long motto): The world may be someone else's oyster. But it's your *toilet!*

How to Handle
Boredom

It might be a good idea at this point to take stock of where you are in your new life as a family dog. And so I've devised a daily work and activity schedule for you. What I did was break the twenty-four-hour day into eight three-hour segments. Then, I carefully considered exactly what important duty or function would most likely be yours during each of these eight periods.

Now I do realize that no two dogs are exactly alike, and on the surface it would seem presumptuous to guess exactly what a canine such as yourself would be doing at any given time. But take my word for it, the schedule that follows will conform exactly to your lifestyle, as it does to mine.

Daily Work and Activity Schedule for an Average House Dog

Time Period	What You Will Probably Be Doing
12:01 A.M.–3:00 A.M.	Nothing
3:01–6:00 A.M.	Nothing
6:01–9:00 A.M.	Nothing
9:01 A.M.–12:00 noon	Nothing
12:01–3:00 P.M.	Nothing
3:01–6:00 P.M.	Nothing
6:01–9:00 P.M.	Nothing
9:01–12:00 P.M.	Nothing

Even when this schedule is broken up occasionally by eating and walking, the fact still remains that a dog's life is unquestionably *the* most boring one since the dawn of civilization. So what it all boils down to is this: How can you best cope with all those excruciatingly endless hours?

First of all, it's already been established that you will sleep twenty hours a day. Which means that over 80 percent of each twenty-four-hour period is already taken care of, right? No way! Your life is so stiflingly dull that even sleep can be boring. So what you have to do is liven it up by sleeping around. (You may not know it, but the expression "sleeping around" has a sexual connotation for humans. But relax, I'm not talking about your sex life here. You can worry about sex later—unless you're introduced to a vet with a sharp knife. In which case you'll have nothing to worry about in that department—ever.)

When I say "sleeping around," I mean purely and simply varying your sleeping spots. Forget that cute little bed basket with the funny flowered mattress and the rubber bone, which they inconveniently set up for you near the back door in the laundry room. Instead, try dropping off on staircases, in the middle of the kitchen floor, in closets, or in open drawers. Then once the thrill wears off, step up your adventurous spirit and start to sleep dangerously.

Try curling up near swinging den doors, in front of

moving vacuum cleaners, at the entrance to bathrooms, near the fireplace, on the mantel on top of the fireplace, *in* the fireplace. Be creative. When somebody asks you a question like, "Hey, you dumb dog, why are you sleeping in the sink with your tail a quarter of an inch away from the garbage disposal unit?" be prepared to say (at least to yourself), "Because it's there!"

During the four hours of the day when you are awake, there are many things you can do to help while away the time. Snorting can be fun for a bit; so is chewing on a furniture leg, or rolling over on your back to dislodge the odd flea. Then there is one of the more interesting canine pastimes: scratching. Start with the tail and then move up to your ear, then reverse the process. This may take care of only forty-six seconds of a three-hour segment, but don't forget, every little bit counts. To help kill the rest of the minute, you might also want to try a fourteen-second spell of yawning, but that's optional and strictly up to you.

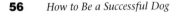

Finally, for something slightly more time-consuming and inventive, think about creative staring. I realize staring in itself is no great, complicated feat. But if you can learn to do it correctly, it can be a true art form.

The steps are simple enough. You hunch up on the floor at your owner's feet. Then you plant your eyes on him and you never take them away. Trust me when I say that it helps immensely if you don't blink. Do this for long stretches and the time will literally melt away.

When should you stop staring at him and find another pastime? Some time right after he starts to squirm and checks to see if his fly is open, and some time right before he throws an orthopedic shoe at you.

6

Satisfying the Inner Dog

WOOOOOOOOOOOOOOOF!

It's time to turn now to perhaps the most gratifying part of a dog's life. No, silly, we're not getting into sex yet, so put your eyes back in your head and keep your tongue in your mouth. I'm referring to eating and drinking.

To a dog owner the whole meal process is cut and dried. She fills your dish with what she considers to be nourishing sustenance, either once or twice a day. She then walks away, expecting you to lap it up and gulp it down, only to go back to sleep and wait for your next feeding. So much for mealtime as far as *she's* concerned. How little she knows and how much you are about to learn.

In actuality a dog's mealtime has no beginning and no end. It's a constant, eternal process, much like the rise and fall of the sun and the ebb and flow of the tides. Eating is a full-time business, make no mistake about it. But being at a disadvantage (as a dog you have no access to pantry shelves or Safeway shopping bags), you must do an incredible amount of improvising.

There are several approaches a dog may take to the dining procedure. For a newcomer like yourself, I suggest something not only uncomplicated, but proven through the years to be highly effective. I'm referring to what, for want of a better phrase, is called the Grand Sweep. Very simply the Grand Sweep works as follows:

You begin your operation at one corner of the kitchen floor (any corner will do) and then turn yourself into a living vacuum cleaner, your legs supplying the power and your mouth the suction. Gradually and thoroughly you clean the kitchen floor from one side to the other. Then, when the procedure is finished, you repeat it indefinitely.

It is amazing how you will learn to incorporate into your daily diet such exotic household delicacies as lint, fuzz, buttons, and roaches, always adhering to the cardinal rule: If it moves (or even if it doesn't), *eat it*!

When you have mastered this process, you are probably

ready to move up from rags to riches. I'm alluding, of course, to that rarefied atmosphere where the name of the game is table food.

As you may have guessed, table food is the stuff that humans eat, and with the possible exception of the bill of fare at three or four dozen fast-food houses in town, it is certainly more desirable than rusty paper clips, torn Brillo pads, dead ants, or a hairball.

The idea then is to separate your owners from some of the table food they may be eating. Which, considering the

overweight, gluttonous slobs they probably are, will be no small accomplishment. In essence, the food is there on the table, they've got it, and you want it. What do you do?

I am not going to play cute games with you or go into complicated psychological ploys. There is *one* way and one way only to get it. But a brief preface before we go into it.

As you may know, being dogs, we don't have to worry about such congenital afflictions as pride and dignity, which have plagued humans since time began. For them, saving face and preserving their integrity are ingrained and as vital as existence itself. To us dogs, the words "pride" and "dignity" are just a lot of gibberish and are about as important as having another tail.

In other words, when you see that table food just crying out to be taken from your owners, there's no act or movement too demeaning or degrading if it can help you accomplish the task. Whine, whimper, cringe, throw yourself abjectly at their feet, keeping in mind that you could never debase yourself too much anyway!

If what is required to land anything from a Mallomar to a chunk of veal parmigiana is to sit up and beg, beg as if your life depended on it, as if you were a wino who hadn't had a thing in his belly for over three weeks. Subjugate yourself totally to your owner, making yourself the most nauseatingly sycophantic creature on earth. If it is in any

way possible to improve your begging technique by putting on a pair of dark glasses and holding out a tin cup with pencils—by all means do it!

A word of advice: If you think there is another way of accomplishing this without self-abasement, by using some secret shortcut that other dogs don't know about, you've got to be pretty damn stupid. So stupid and naïve, in fact, that it's hardly worth wasting any more words on a lop-eared, four-legged nincompoop like yourself. So do me a favor, idiot, and drop dead!

If you have even an ounce of insight, you probably realize now that that outburst I unleashed was just a test to check your psychological makeup. If what I said bothered you at all—even in an infinitesimal way—I'm afraid you may be suffering from a slight touch of pride and dignity. It grieves me to inform you that there is no way you can ever engage successfully in full-scale table food manipulation. What I suggest you do is face reality, live with your infirmity, and settle for a lifetime diet of bugs and dirt because, frankly, that's all you're going to get. However, if the paragraph didn't annoy you in the least—happy dining! You've got some terrific eating years ahead of you.

One last word on the subject. Don't ever worry about your diet. As a dog, you are physically equipped to digest just about anything. But there is one thing you should *never* eat—dog food!

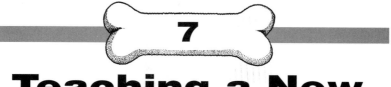

7

Teaching a New Dog Old Tricks

I think it should be clear at this stage of the book that I am being totally candid with you at all times. I've laid it on the line and I've pulled no punches. I fervently believe—and I trust you agree with me—that this honest approach will help immeasurably in making you a better dog. Which is merely an introduction to what I am about to say, something that I hope you will accept in the right way.

To a pet owner, a dog is really a young child, with one notable exception. Real children have a tendency to grow up, mature, and perhaps in time

take over. Dogs do no such thing, of course. We may grow physically, but we mature minimally: my job is to try to build up your maturation level.

Assuming that you're one of those dogs with the kind of "pride and dignity" problem mentioned in the last chapter, allow the shock to wear off, and then let's concentrate on happier things. The good news is that, since you are likened to a child, very little is expected of you. In other words, there is practically no pressure on you to do anything too important. So whatever you *do* do above and beyond barking and tail wagging is truly monumental to your master.

Which brings us to the area of dog "tricks." (I put quotes around the word "tricks" for a specific reason—dog tricks are about as complex and difficult for a canine to master as sneezing while walking through a pepper patch with a bad cold.) But the fact remains that, along with "cute," nothing is more important to the average owner than to have a pet do tricks.

Without question, some time early on in your tenure as a house dog you too will be brought forward to center stage and asked to perform. How you handle yourself from that point on can play a vital part in your entire development process and can actually mean the difference between a good life and a tolerable existence.

All right, let's assume your owner says to you, "Come on, pooch, let's see what you can do. Give me your paw." Now, giving someone your paw is not exactly in the same cerebral category as translating Nietzsche from the original German text. So, to prove that you're a lot brighter than your owner even *dreamed* you were, what you do is not only give your paw, but you roll over, sit up and beg, play dead, and fetch sticks for seven hours—*right???*

If you agree to that, you're not stupid—you're demented!

Are you questioning my judgment? Okay, let's assume you put on a dazzling display of canine prestidigitation. Let's say you wow them with your fetching ability, you slay them with your ball retrieving, you kill them with your rolling over, sitting up, playing dead, catching 124 Frisbees in a row with your molars, and so on. Let's assume you do all that and more to thunderous applause, leaving them limp with excitement and exploding with pride. Terrific! But when the cheering finally subsides, ask yourself this question: What am I going to do for them tomorrow?

You see, bubby, it's like this: Unless you can keep topping yourself every day (and believe me, you can't), you've got no place to go but down!

And so it may not be a bad idea to borrow from an earlier chapter. Remember what I said about your daily walks? Hold off on your bodily functions as long as possible because once you commit yourself to both, you're back in the house like a rocket—not only a disappointed dog but a dead duck! Once again the answer here is: Delay, delay, delay.

Let's say your master commands you to sit. Now this is a trick that is just a little bit tougher for you than breath-

ing. Nevertheless, what you do is look quizzically for a half hour or so, circle a spot on the floor, start to sink, then stop, and slowly and carefully lean over and start to scratch your crotch. In about six months (if you don't die of boredom first, pretending you're as dumb as your owners think you are), you can finally sit on command.

Since they'll probably celebrate this momentous event with a three-week block party, you should have a long respite before they move you on to your next trick. And when they do, you should know how to proceed accordingly.

Just for the record, here is a chart listing five typical dog tricks with some important time projections for you to study:

The Trick	How Long It Should Really Take You to Master It	How Long You Should Pretend It Takes You
Giving your paw	3½ seconds	14 months
Rolling over	¾ of a second	2½ to 3 years
Fetching newspapers in your mouth	1¾ minutes	5 years
Playing dead	2 seconds	6 to 7 years
Standing on your hind legs	8 minutes	14 years

Giving your paw

Rolling over

Fetching newspapers in your mouth

Playing dead

Standing on your hind legs

In summing up, it is imperative that you dole out all so-called tricks in very small portions. Convince your master that you're practically a helpless dolt and that any minus-cule action on your part, like coughing or panting, should be welcomed as a small miracle. Believe me—then you'll have it made! But a word of warning: You may very well blow the whole thing if you're caught reading this book! I know, because my owner just caught me *writing* it!

Have Leash, Will Travel

Until now, the only things we have dealt with that involve your behavior *away* from the house have been your daily walks. We are now ready to discuss how to act on longer trips—extended journeys covering four or five miles, or even farther.

I realize that five miles doesn't sound like a big deal, but think . . . when you apply the principle that every *human* year is equivalent to seven *dog* years, a five-mile trip with your master could be like thirty-five miles for you. Come to think of it, thirty-five miles is still no big deal! Okay, wise guy, I'd like to see you come up with brilliant ideas when *you* get to be 20 years old like me (and that goes for your smart-ass master when *he's* 140!).

When I refer to longer trips I mean, of course, auto travel. (As for air travel, unless your master has a Marquis de Sade complex and enjoys incarcerating you in a cage in the hold of some jet between skis and a duffel bag with eight pairs of rumpled chinos, forget it.)

There is nothing complex or mystifying about how a dog should act during an auto trip. You could do most of it with your eyes closed. And since your eyes are closed twenty hours a day anyway (if your eyes are open, see chapter 5, "How to Handle Boredom"), it's a bigger piece of cake than you imagined.

First of all, regardless of how many humans there are in the auto, never situate yourself on any part of the car seat itself. You must *always* sit in somebody's lap, whether you think they want you there or not—and believe me, they don't.

All right, let's assume you're now seated in the driver's lap, impairing her vision and movement and making her a more dangerous loaded weapon in a car than if she had three quarts of bourbon in her craw. Your next step is a minor trigonometry exercise. Specifically, using your seat as one corner of an isosceles triangle, you must extend your olfactory organ to a position equilateral to the ozone layer of . . .

But why am I wasting my time getting scientific with someone who hardly knows how to pant after chasing a squirrel for 300 yards? What I'm trying to say is, you must find a way to stick your nose out of an open window and start sniffing like crazy.

Why is sniffing through an open window so vital to a traveling dog? Because if you don't, you miss out on inhaling the exhaust fumes of 8,200 passing cars. There are other reasons, but that one is important enough.

You may or may not know an old saying regarding man and bread, but I'll paraphrase it anyway: A dog in transit does not live by sniffing alone. So it is therefore imperative to punctuate those sniffs with extended salvos of barking. However (and I can't overemphasize the importance of this), you bark only during either one of these occurrences:

1. When there is another dog in a car that goes past yours;
2. When there is not.

So much for vehicles in motion. At one time or another the car you are in is going to stop. And when it does, there is an 85 percent chance that everybody is going to get out—except *you.*

How you act alone in a parked car may be the most monumental test of your worth as a dog, and could well influence the success or failure of not only you, but your descendants for centuries to come. (Did I just frighten the hell out of you with that apocalyptic palaver? Relax. Actually, it's no more important than learning how to scratch your ear. I realize education doesn't come easy to you; I just have to jar you every once in a while to make sure you're paying attention.)

Before leaving you behind in the car, the first thing your owners will probably do is open the window a crack so that you don't suffocate. We already know the quality of the air outside the car, so your chances of survival immediately drop 12 percent compared with what they might have been had they forgotten and left you sealed in.

Left alone in the car now, your modus operandi is as follows: Seek and destroy! This is an ideal time for dietary experimentation. We've already established in an earlier chapter that you'll eat anything in the house. Well, now's the time to expand your culinary horizons. You must paw, bite, rip, and chew everything in sight. This includes window adornments,

such as oversized dice and baby shoes; radio knobs; audiocassettes (the loose tape can be eaten like pasta); windshield wiper buttons; and so on. It will absolutely amaze you, for example, to discover what a gustatory delight seat covers can be when mixed to taste with cigarette butts.

Once the animal in you has been allowed to expend its physical and digestive fury, it is time for the aesthetic side to take over. I'm referring to your artistic nature.

Naturally, we dogs are unequipped for finger painting, but God atoned for this shortcoming by blessing us with the talent for tongue painting.

A word or two on this highly esoteric art: your canvas, as you may have guessed, is the back, front, and side win-

dows of the car. You proceed to make your artistic statement with broad horizontal tongue strokes across the glass (vertical, to finish off the corners). *Voilà*, you call your canvas *Autumn Sunset*.

Quick Quiz: *How will you know if your painting is a success?*

Answer: If the *real* autumn sunset hits one of the smudged windows and you can't see it.

Finally, if the purpose of your owner's stop was to pick up a case of white wine, when she returns to the car and sees the condition you left it in, she will probably chuckle

MURPHY

HE ATE OUR MEAT
HE ATE OUR BREAD
HE ATE OUR CAR
AND NOW HE'S DEAD

and call you a "mischievous little mutt." However, if she stopped at a used car lot to sell the auto and returns with a prospective buyer, she won't have time to call you anything. She'll be too busy strangling you.

9

Protecting Your Turf

If someone were to take a poll to determine what the most exciting term in the English language is, chances are the expression "house dog" not only wouldn't make the Top Ten, but would have to struggle to make the Top Thousand. I still maintain, however, that we canines who share that much maligned appellation have nothing to be ashamed of; nay, we have every right to flaunt it.

Because, you see, unlike many turgid and pretentious expressions, "house dog," if nothing else, says it like it is. In essence, a house dog is just that—the dog of the house, and with that title come certain unwritten rights, territorial and otherwise.

One of the foremost tasks throughout your—hopefully—illustrious career as a dog will be to protect your turf. And you must know how to do that properly.

Let's assume a visitor has come to the house. Now, the fact that he (or she) is there to see another human (your owner or whoever) should in no way preclude you from immediately letting the caller know about *your* power position in the household, as well as your territorial rights. In short, you must make it clear that you are not just some inconsequential four-legged nonentity, but an important force to be dealt with.

When protecting your turf, here is the step-by-step process to follow:

1. Confront the visitor.
2. Look him (or her) directly in the eye.
3. Bark like hell.
4. Stop to allow the full expression of your authority to sink in, leaving the visitor completely awed and

quaking in his (or her) shoes by the sheer physical presence of so formidable a canine as yourself.

5. Go to sleep by a flowerpot.

In truth, barking is the only method you have of asserting your authority in the house. So use it wisely, effectively, and with discretion. For example, you *must* bark during the following occurrences:

1. When the doorbell rings;
2. When a police siren or ambulance siren sounds;
3. When there is a thunderstorm;

4. When another dog barks in front of your house;

5. When another dog barks halfway down the block;

6. When another dog barks around the corner;

7. When another dog barks in Kankakee, Illinois (unless you *live* in Kankakee—in which case bark twice).

So much for occurrences. I am now going to list those callers at the door whom you should and should *not* bark at. I would advise tearing out this list and keeping it in a safe place for constant reference.

Those You Should Bark At

Amway representatives

cable guys

mail deliverers

Avon ladies

newspaper deliverers

magazine vendors

meter readers

TV repairmen

Federal Express carriers

visiting neighbors

fund-raisers

plumbers

Jehovah's Witnesses

Seventh Day Adventists
Six-day bike riders
Five-card-stud players
Four Horsemen of the Apocalypse
Three Musketeers
Two Gentlemen of Verona
and A Partridge in a Pear Tree

Those You Should Never Bark At

burglars

Callers at the door aside, earlier in the chapter we talked about one kind of visitor who actually sets paws inside your house, and by this time you should know exactly how to deal with him. We are now going to discuss an entirely different type of in-house visitor. Obviously, the fact that you have a strong and natural emotional tie to him won't make your task any easier.

I'm alluding, of course, to *another dog*. Yes, every so often some presumptuous human will dare to bring a canine along on a visit. Please pay careful attention now to the following:

If you recall, earlier in the book, I mentioned the fact that there is never room in a successful dog's life for pride and dignity. Well, change that "never" to "hardly ever." In this case pride and dignity are *sine qua nons*.

You have every right to be proud of your domicile. And you also have every right to take pride in your personal position in the household. An interloper (if even a four-legged *temporary* one) should be made keenly aware of this.

What you must do to put the intruding dog in his or her rightful place is similar (up to a point) to how you would act with a human visitor. The confrontation, the hard stare, and—naturally—the barking. But in addition to all this, you must assume an air of dignity. You must approach the visitor with dignity; you must circle your turf

with dignity; then (and here comes the difficult part) you must wet the floor with dignity.

(I have often been asked by fledgling dogs like yourself, as well as by more seasoned ones, why we canines always wet the floor when another dog enters our household. I'll give you my answer, but it's going to be painful. The answer is: I don't know!)

Still, the fact remains that when other dogs enter the home, the Big Dog Upstairs gives us secret cues and we wet the floor.

And so, to sum up this segment of the chapter, a successful dog confronts visiting dogs, stares at them, barks at them, and then minds his cues and pees.

A final word on the subject now. It is important that we address ourselves to another ghastly possibility. Namely, the intruding canine may not belong to a visitor, and he or she may not be dropping by temporarily. You've heard of two-car families? Need I say more?

If indeed the new dog is ensconced as a permanent member of the household, sharing billing with you, you have one of three choices to make as far as your behavior is concerned:

1. You can accept the new dog as an equal and maintain peace and harmony in the house.
2. You can fight to the death for territorial rights.
3. You can continuously pretend that the new dog is really just a temporary visitor, always to be treated like any other dog who invades your turf. In which case the house will eventually float away on a sea of pee.

10

The Fine Art of Living with Guilt

As you recall, at the very beginning of this book, I painstakingly pointed out the vast differences between dogs and our blood enemies: cats. We discussed things like contrasting lifestyles, dissimilar temperaments, and so on. Well, in addition to all we have covered, we dogs have yet another character trait that is completely alien to the

feline. And it can best be demonstrated in the following situation:

Let's assume that a cat owner returns one night after a hard day at the office. He looks down at his highly valued living room carpet—all scratched and chewed to shreds, looking more like egg foo yung than a Chinese antique rug.

As if this weren't bad enough, the cat owner then discovers that despite his openmouthed horror, screams, and blatant hysteria, the feline culprit leisurely continues her destruction job! Caught red-pawed, she continues to polish off the remainder of the rug. Casually brushing the fabric hairs from her whiskers, she looks up at her master and, with a face of total innocence, appears to say, "Okay, I'm finished. Can I have my fortune cookie now?" Getting no response, she sniffs haughtily and slinks off to another room.

Now let's take a parallel situation in a canine home. A dog owner enters his bedroom and finds the remains of his

favorite slipper in his dog's mouth. Will he similarly get an indifferent or hostile response from his pet? Not on your flea-bitten life!

The dog immediately stops chewing, panic builds in his eyes, his heart begins pumping wildly, and then he slowly rolls over on his back, paws extended helplessly in the air, and his tail begins wagging furiously.

What is the dog trying to say through this pathetically demeaning series of gestures? Something more or less like this: "Oh, my God, I just did something terrible, and I can't express to you how sorry I am! Here I am at your mercy to do with as you please. Hit me! Beat me! Torture me! Whatever you do, I deserve it!"

I trust you get the point. Specifically, one other unique facet of canine psychological makeup is our ability to demonstrate guilt. This is practically unheard of in cats and most other four-legged beasts (many two-legged ones as well).

Remember that word: "guilt." It will play such an important part in your life that it might as well be engraved on your rabies-shot tag! And since *no* creature can display guilt as effectively and brilliantly as a dog, learn your art and learn it well.

Sure, I can hear the cynics out there among you barking, "What's so tough about demonstrating guilt? All animals or humans with a conscience [and we dogs definitely have consciences] can easily show shame when we do something wrong."

Ah-ha, you inadvertently hit the bull's-eye with the phrase "when we do something wrong." Perhaps a minority of other creatures somewhere can show guilt when they do something wrong. But here's where we stand alone: We dogs must know how to display guilt even when we're *totally innocent!*

Let's set up another hypothetical "dog owner and pet" situation. Your owner walks into the kitchen and finds a trash pail overturned, with garbage strewn all over the floor. What she does know is that the place is a horrid mess. What she doesn't know, however, is that you were in a back room for the past thirty-seven hours (establishing a new nonstop sleeping record) and that you haven't set paw in the kitchen in two days! She goes up to you, twin jets of flame shooting from her eyes, drags you by an ear over to the mess, and shouts, "What did you do? What did you *do!?!?*"

All right now, how would you react to *that* set of circumstances? The answer is simple: You will automatically roll over on your back, extend your paws helplessly in the air, and start wagging your tail furiously.

What will you be saying through this series of gestures? The gist of it is more or less as follows: "Oh, my God, I didn't do *anything* wrong, but I can't tell you how sorry I am anyway. I accept total responsibility for what happened, no matter *who* did it."

Here then is the story of a dog's moral life in a nutshell: Whether we're guilty or innocent, we're guilty!

Sound strange? The reasoning a bit convoluted? Maybe. But there is a very definite historical (make that biblical) precedent for a dog's inherent guilt complex, and I think it is important to mention it before closing out this chapter.

It all started at the very beginning of time—about two thousand years ago. In the so-called Beginning, there was a tree in the Garden of Eden, from which God specifically forbade the picking of fruit. Well, as it happened, a snake talked Eve, the world's first woman, into picking an apple from the tree anyway. This led to the Original Sin, which was in time transmitted to the entire human race.

So much for people. Now, where do we canines get all our guilt from?

Well, that very tree we were just talking about, from which Eve picked the forbidden fruit and triggered all the evil on earth as we know it today . . . *was planted by a dog!*

You don't believe it? You think it sounds preposterous? Listen, buster, if a snake can talk, a dog can plant!

11

Expressing Emotions

Expanding on the subject of guilt, I am now briefly going to compare dogs not to cats this time, but to human beings, in order to make an important point. And it all has to do with emotions in general.

For the record, the dictionary describes the word "emotion" as an "affective state of consciousness, in which joy, sorrow, fear, hate, or the like is experienced . . . usually accompanied by certain physiological changes, such as increased heartbeat or respiration, and often overt manifestations, such as crying, shaking, or laughing."

I would now like you to look at the facing page and study a whole spectrum of typical human emotions as projected by an average group of people.

Now look below and see a dog running his own gamut of emotions. You can see the dog displaying, among other things, happiness, fear, anticipation, trepidation, uncertainty, anxiety, love, excitement, eagerness, confusion, irritation, panic, and nervousness.

Sorry I had to lay that one on you, kiddo. But I think you should have gotten the point: As far as a dog's ability to express his feelings is concerned, the tail says it all. And without our tails we'd be eternally relegated to the Emotionally Handicapped Parking Spot of Life.

However, due to the extreme complexity of the tail and the magnitude of its emotional spectrum, serious problems may occur, and how you handle them can determine your very existence.

FADDA
FADDA
FAT FAT
FAT......

A case in point: I once knew a mild-mannered German Shepherd named Sheldon, who witnessed a vicious street fight between a gargantuan Saint Bernard and a humongous Great Dane. As Sheldon looked on, his tail began wagging furiously. This infuriated the Saint Bernard, who had taken a fearful beating.

"What's with your tail?" barked the Saint Bernard through his bloody teeth (he had a loose molar, and this canine had lost a canine).

"I'm a born pacifist," barked Sheldon. "This terrible battle makes me nervous and panicky. I fear you will tear each other limb from limb. Peace, brothers, peace!"

"That's funny," the Saint Bernard barked back. "I thought you were wagging your tail because you were happy I got my ass kicked in."

"That's not true," a terrified Sheldon barked. "I swear," he added, kissing his paw up to heaven.

But the wounded Saint Bernard ignored the protest, leaped at Sheldon, and began to dismantle him with his remaining teeth. He ripped out all of the German Shepherd's hair, stretched his ears, and cut him down to 10 percent of his former body size. The Saint Bernard then walked off wagging his own tail, expressing excitement, eagerness, and paranoia.

And here's where a brutally battered Sheldon reached

the crossroads of his life. He could have whined "Why me?" considered himself an innocent victim, and run off to join the poor homeless dogs on the street, living from paw to mouth, begging bones from passing butchers.

Fortunately, Sheldon was made of sterner and more resourceful stuff.

When his wounds healed, he looked at himself in a mirror, assessing his bare back, his elongated floppy ears, and his drastically reduced body size. "I'm not a German Shepherd anymore," he barked fatalistically. Then he was hit by a sudden revelation: "But I *could* be a Chihuahua."

To make a long story (and a long dog) short, today the former Sheldon has kennels on both coasts, a gold-encrusted dinner bowl, and is making a bloody fortune doing taco commercials on television.

You should be so smart—and so lucky.

12

Facing Up
to Punishment

Regardless of how harmonious your relationship with your owner may be, certain instances are bound to turn up periodically in which (rightly or wrongly) you will be subjected to some form of chastisement. Perhaps you have destroyed a valuable cushion or piece of furniture, or had a momentary lapse in bodily function control.

Sooner or later you're bound to get it, and dog punishment, like everything else in this world, can manifest itself in many different ways. However, I can safely say from my vantage point of experience that there is a 95 percent chance yours will encompass one, two, or all three of the following time-tested classic forms.

The Verbal Assault

As the expression connotes, this is by and large an oral tirade consisting of gibberish such as, "You bad dog, what did you do? . . . Shame on you, you naughty puppy! . . . Don't you *dare* do that again!" and so on, ad nauseam. This form of punishment seems to be innocuous enough and simple to handle. But beware. This could probably lead to a physical barrage on your body, including the laying on of hands, or worse yet, leashes across the flank, and other eventualities too unspeakable to mention.

What you must do in the face of a verbal assault is pretend that it has penetrated your deepest sensitivity layers, that your feelings are shattered, and—here is where your true acting prowess comes to the fore—that you're scared to death of those idiotic words.

Specifically, upon receiving the verbal assault, do not make any one of the following faux pas:

1. Treat it indifferently because you know—pardon the expression—it's all bark and no bite.
2. Concentrate on something else, like scratching your crotch, during the tirade.
3. Horrors of horrors, yawning in your owner's face out of total, consuming boredom.

The Journalistic Castigation

Once, during a rather odd moment in history, an anonymous dog owner (probably secretly against freedom of the press) awoke from a deep sleep with what he believed to be an invention of Edisonian proportions. He rose from his creative slumber and introduced a new, efficacious

method of punishing his errant dog—battering the beast with a rolled-up newspaper! Needless to say, it caught on like Beanie Babies! The automotive section of the daily newspaper has become the pet owner's *ultimate weapon!*

Now, if you've ever been on the receiving end of a standard newspaper swat, you know of course that the pain inflicted is only a modicum more intense than a fusillade of marshmallows being hurled against the sides of a rogue elephant. So once again pretense is in order.

The Big Dipper

Some time after the rolled-up newspaper invention, another dog owner grew tired of his pet's recalcitrance in following house-breaking rules. Sick of having to scoop up offensive deposits from the floor, this master came up with a brilliant punishment idea of his own (or so he thought), which has since become *de rigueur* in just about every dog owner's private training manual.

In essence his thesis was: Make the pet pay for his social blunder by shoving his face in it. However, the perspicacious inventor of this slice of ingenuity forgot one important thing. We dogs have some rather bizarre dietary habits (which, you may recall, we've already discussed). This leads to the following important bit of advice:

If and when your owners catch you in a bodily function mishap in the house and proceed to shove your face into it, you must not—repeat, must *not*—let them know you're enjoying it!

13

Everything You Have to Know About Sex— So Why Ask

If you remember, a few chapters back the subject of sex came up, and I told you that you could worry about it later. Well, this is later! And there's really nothing to worry about. Except *one* thing.

Some time early in your tenure as a house dog, perhaps in your second or third month of life, your owner may come up with the idea of

imposing the ultimate indignity on you. She may decide that you're a prime candidate for—as the classic euphemism goes—"getting fixed." What makes the expression so ludicrous is that the only way anyone can fix anything is if it's broken. And how can you break something if they never let you use it?

If you do happen to be "fixed," I suggest you skip this chapter, increase your daily sleep schedule to 23½ hours, and take up modeling for dog food commercials!

But let's assume—happily— that you don't have to make that dreaded trip to the vet and that you're allowed to maintain full use of your apparatus. All you have to know are a few basic things, and then it's smooth sailing. To begin with, another comparison between us and people is in order.

To humans "sex" has always been a buzzword and is charged with all kinds of dangerous currents. The mere *mention* of the word conjures up a myriad of loaded expressions for them, terms like "physically attractive," "mutual interests," "the same wavelength," "pressure to perform," "not in the mood," "you'll lose respect for me in the morning," "please be gentle," "I've never done this before," "let's get kinky," and "I'm not *that* kind!"

Without reviewing the specific details, for humans to even *anticipate* a sexual adventure, they go through laborious preparation, intricate plans, and inordinate strategies. Regardless of the eventual result, all of it often leads to exhaustion, depression, guilt, fear, and confusion! What fun, right?

For us, sex is not nearly that complicated.

Just for the record, here are some of the things dogs *don't* have to do for sex:

1. Buy flowers.

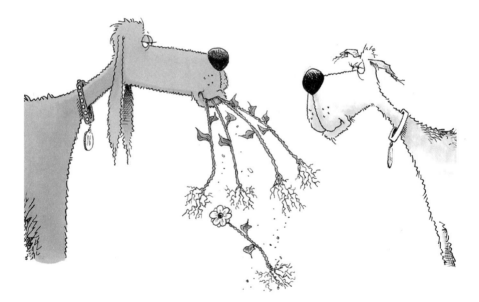

2. Strum a guitar in the moonlight outside a kennel.

3. Share a magnum of champagne in a pair of water bowls.

4. Engage in meaningless small-bark.

5. And, finally, when it's over, try to light a couple of cigarettes with your paws.

On the other paw, dogs have only *two* things to be concerned with: timing and climbing!

I can practically hear some of you bitches out there right now growling, "What kind of crap is that? We're not sexual objects, *things!* It wouldn't kill some of you flea-infested studs if maybe you did romance us once in a while instead of always sniffing around! And who are you calling 'bitches' anyway?"

Simmer down, girls! Nobody's claiming that you're sexual objects! If it were at all possible, there's nothing we male dogs would like better than to take you driving in the back of a pickup truck and dine on milk bones at some little, out-of-the-way pet shop. But you know our limitations! For God's sake, *we* didn't write the sexual rules for canines.

You feel insulted? You want revenge on males? You're in the wrong racket. Become a praying mantis. They devour their partners after sex!

As for calling you "bitches," boy, are you touchy! "Bitch" is a perfectly innocuous word. Look it up in Webster. It means "female dog." (*Humans* are the ones who've given it a vile connotation.) Mark my word, some day we dogs are going to make them pay for that and a lot of other things. I'll be a son of a woman if we don't.

But I've digressed enough. You already know all you have to know about sex. It's out there. Go get it.

Just in case some of you male dogs also have complaints regarding those sexual rules we just discussed, look at the bright side. As I've already said, compared to humans, everything we do can be multiplied in time by seven. So, if it bothers you that the act itself takes you only one second, merely multiply one by seven, and what you really get is a fantastic sexual endurance time of *seven seconds!* Hmmm, I guess you're not too thrilled. . . .

Look, don't bug me. I've got a cat book to write, and I've wasted enough time on nonprofit work.

Epilogue

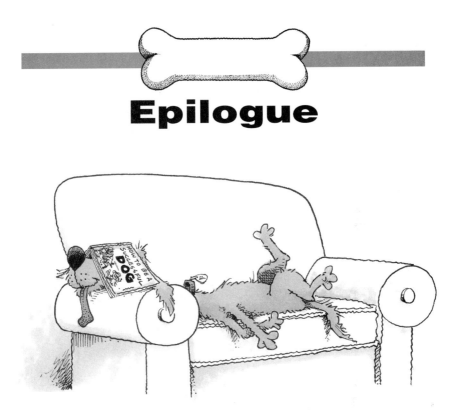

In conclusion, I hope that this book represents to all you dogs the single most important experience of your heretofore humdrum and highly unproductive existence. Among many other things, I fervently pray that my treatise has unmistakably opened your eyes and shown you that there are far more important things in this world to concentrate on than sleeping your life away.

But I've sermonized and lectured you long enough. It's your turn to speak to me.

Any volunteers?

How about Matisse, that fuzzy white bichon frise out there in California, who has roots of nobility dating back to sixteenth-century French royalty?

Speak, noble canine! Express your heartfelt feelings for this book, the chef d'oeuvre of my life. Speak for all of dogdom!

Zzzzzzzzzzzzzzzzzzzzzzzzzzzzzzzzzz!

About the Author

The remarkable writing career of Larry Siegel took root in the mid-1940s, when he returned home from Europe, having won a very important war with the help of his 10th Mountain Division buddy Bob Dole, and a few other American soldiers.

He enrolled at the University of Illinois, where he edited the school humor magazine, *Shaft*, replacing the then unknown Hugh Hefner. Hefner strongly resented being displaced by Siegel, but the latter won him over by helping Hef get dates.

In the fifties, the editors of *MAD* came across one of Siegel's funniest early pieces in "Nuts and Bolts," the house organ of a combination candy shop and hardware store in Passaic, New Jersey. The article was a brilliant personal portrait of his beloved aunt called "Rivke—The Years of Angst." It was at that moment that the *MAD* editors knew they had struck gold.

Siegel proceeded to write a few hundred pieces for *MAD* over the years, including such movie parodies as "The Oddfather," "Flawrence of Arabia," and "Balmy and Clod," and his now legendary bit of Americana humor called "Eli Eli," which was a hilarious portrait of Mr. Whitney, the madcap inventor of the cotton gin. In addition, Siegel has written four books for Warner. He was also "satirist in residence" for *Playboy* for several years until he was finally convinced to stop by the Editorial Board, when Hef agreed to get *him* dates.

In the 1960s, Siegel and Stan Hart, another *MAD* idiot, cowrote *The* MAD *Show*. It ran on the New York stage for two years, until it was finally caught by the authorities, and the entire production, including the props and scenery, was shackled and remanded to the Mattewan Hospital for the Criminally Insane.

From the seventies until the present day, Siegel has been selling film scripts to Warner Bros., MGM, and sundry other studios. He also wrote for Carol Burnett, *Laugh-In*, and many other TV shows. Thus far he has received three Emmys for writing, as well as the highly coveted Friendliest Writer in America Award from the Carnegie Institute.

For the record, Siegel has also taught classes at UCLA and has acted on stage, in films, and in commercials. But despite his incredible success, his lifelong dream has still not been realized—namely, to own and operate his own unicycle repair shop in Bemidji, Minnesota.

About the Illustrator

John Caldwell is a regular contributor to *MAD* Magazine. He lives in upstate New York with his wife, Diane, and his dog, Britt—who has mixed feelings about her owner having anything to do with a book featuring other dogs, many of whom are much less successful than herself.